ARCHITECTURE OF INTERIOR SPACE

AND

THE SIMPLE METHOD OF THREE

BY

ALEXIS STAMATIS

TRANSLATED BY

THOM NAIRN

AND

D. ZERVANOU

ARCHITECTURE OF INTERIOR SPACE AND THE SIMPLE
METHOD OF THREE

This edition published in 2001
by Dionysia Press
20A Montgomery Street
Edinburgh EH7 5JS

Set by Dionysia Press

ISBN: 1 903171 05 9

Dionysia Press would like to express thanks to the European
Commission's Ariane programme for financial support in the publication
of this work.

Work translated with the support of the European Commission's Ariane
programme

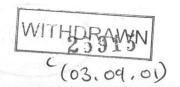

CONTENTS

ARCHITECTURE OF INTERIOR SPACE

THE SIMPLE METHOD OF THREE

ARCHITECTURE OF INTERIOR SPACE

To Pauline

THE SWIMMING POOL

As I swim through my dreams
dictated by the night
in the red stone swimming pool
beneath midnight stars
stars both great and small
I swim
I stare at myself in the floor of the pool
not breathing in the void
the garden becomes a sky
and I witness my translucent memories
shattered into splinters
in the grooves furrowing my skin
I see
time blowing through the buildings
as my body like a glider blends
with these forms
a lost whisper
in the weird fragrance of the dawn
when the mouth's victim becomes still.

HATRED

Hatred
pitiless inexorable bitter
deadly and beyond compromise
hatred
and envy
an empathy ingrained
filling me with malice
to seethe and boil
to cultivate
the hideous implaccable
the foul
for the bad demon
la bete humaine
to be envious
of course within the rules of the game
the cherished and intimate game
where the beloved self
stretches
madly loved and hated
seeking the sympathy of weakness.

TAMED BLOOD

The potting clay will illuminate the root and the palm
a cluster of organs will nurture the germination
incarnating the human, the soul will begin to hunt
tamed blood will surge from purified pores
gauging pulse from the sediment.

DEMON

The closet intellectual
whose name was entangled
in the tug of war
was active wide alive
as an originator
a former and manipulator
working the atmosphere of exchange
while the power of "criteria"
acted as a delicate and sensitive factor surreptitiously
serving to form a favourable climate
for the development of profitable activity
until an existentialist shock
like a lightning rod
picked up the idols
and the organism began to be depicted
as a totem
to be run down as a symbol
to be vaporised as a perpetrator
a founder of the indisputable nature of the infamous
a mode of fabrication - a sample of intrigue
as the great debtor of idiosyncracy
despite all connections
is deplored by suspense
suddenly
all at once, here it is, the means.

An absolute comprehension of inertia
of antagonism
a cathartic victim then,
he now has good relations as a private individual
the demon is distanced now
revelling narcistically in his manipulations.

THE DICE

There's no sound
except for the breath
and the murder of the cranium.

The dawn spreads on
the edge of town
like thrown dice
with some three legged animals
braeing and deep in hunger for them.

BLUES AT THE END

The colours stayed red
though the night had already passed
I remember it was a surname that cut me.

Whatever took place is history

light blew and swept it all down in the afternoon.

Now there are bullets in the bath I wash myself
in the depths of the mirror in the heat
I stretch awakening to the sugar
gaping at the falling drops of coffee

that Easter night
the blades were hidden under the pillows
the bed in a half darkness
the moon just found its place
and the room just sat waiting
impatiently
for the dark strokes which fell to the sea
midnight when darkness fell in fear.

Now though there's silence
and calm inside
I withdraw into sleep
the traces on the sheets are still frozen
in those blues at the end.

DOME

The red gouges on his face
open fissures like slatted shutters
cutting, fragmeting, the light of his mind
as at that time in London
there outside the Dome
where just a look
encompassed all of the yesterdays
immaculately transformed into today.

THE LAKE

A

Be wary - he said
in the north of the country there is a lake
and a huge water spout
from which words surge forth
and there is a crank-shaft
which controls the flow
designed to cast them later
to the bed of the lake
where the words are naked
in the heavy vegetation of the depths
where the waters churn incessantly
around diving suits which drift
full of sulphur and bismuth
the diving suits
and the words lean on water-lilies
where the frogs rest at midday

There are rafts too
bound in oakum
which drift moored in cycles
there are masses of bones on the rafts
and anemones
voices emerge from the foam
wet and swollen it is misty
and through the haze voices rise
blood red
from above pale clouds descend
rain falls on the voices
and they cling to the cyclamens
it is night

B

Frequently the waters writhe within
subterraneously you'd think
as if poluted but becoming purified
the banks are displaced
and water-lilies emerge
full of voices and frogs
from the lake an ominous murmuring ascends
a whispering drowned in sobbing
the water in the gullies crumble muddily
climbs to join the land
the sounds embrace the trees
embellishing the branches
the resin gleams
in the blending of water and sound
at night in the swamp and sulphur
when amphibians sharpen their claws on trees
and on their scales tadpoles make branches grow
on the ferns the animals howl
and the wind rages
lightning fills the space
and a figure rises bare breasted
as if sculpted in rock
and stands in the midst of the storm
shivering

C

She is swathed in a sheet
or a robe I cannot make out the clothing
with dishevelled hair she stands in the downpour
and the water shines on her forehead
in the power of the night
she stands

and the lake creeps towards her
sounds embrace her ankles
enwrap her body
the dawn opens all eyes
as the lake crawls closer and closer
in the light and the darkness perishes
as always
when the rhythm of breath breaks the shell
as always
when a black stone appears
the whole lake turns to blood.

NIGHT

A sparkling red sky wrestles with me.
It's the eyes of those
I let pass during the day.
Returning at night.

White walls encircle me.
The dead inside are fire and change
as I chew on the raw balsam
of the five fingers of one love.

My young state no more has a place.
Here the protagonist
seems akin to
death streaming from the nose
the stench from the palm.
It is from there the poison emanates.

You called me an 'Angel'
but it was a failed attempt.
All at once like tiny crumbs
the dark idols picked them up and left.

THE WRITINGS OF SLEEP

The writings I see in my sleep
are so clear, so transparent
as if woven in lace
this is how they visit me as the night grows smaller
and the verbs slide over my body.

I ask you:

What language is this?

You say the unperceived

and you depart to
a cold unwashed room
where a narrow rain drizzles
so the water won't fray
into the dimmest of lights, the universe.

Men of the same country await you there
a place which leaves them empty
empty images of bodies
men are like paragraphs
waiting for you
with the eyes of others.

You, a green and tender Hero, hold to the writings of sleep
firmly between your legs
those ancient legs
so's death doesn't stall on the age
and you sit
with open eyes
your empty space visible to all
at Night when it drifts down black

the horde is rising
to create a white murmuring.

ENCOUNTER

The stone was light blue and alive as I walked the edge
of the kerb loitering when music crept over the ground
it reached up to the kerb and there they all were
assembled looking down as if
ashamed acting like school kids.
It was so funny I forgot for a moment who they were
but I waved to them to come over.
They came each one holding a piece of myself.

8+ ∞

The discs were hard and I grew hard
although my clothes were light.

Memories were revealed and imprinted.

At my command my classmate becomes ashen
beckons to me from the other side
with the thirsty word "come"
from the boundary at the red light
the locked road is slippery
where the trucks empty water.

The issues of love rolled like wheels
blood is the constituent of the asphalt
over the curved 8, the infinite.

EYES AND MOUTH

But I live
eyes and mouth
mouth and eyes
I live
I stretch mirrors over my body
and white and blue pots
gather the fluids
the inactivity of the body is exempt
in the hospitals of the future
in the towns
in the skin-towns
where coffee is drunk all the time
there I drip
I live
mouth and eyes
I grow four legs in the cafes
to drink in fever
to drink from the eyes and mouth
to drink.

THE CARRIAGE OF BLOOD

In the end it all reeks in the dark
unless you feed on the light.
I must remember the earthen shroud
which illuminates and reverses myrrh
towards the sacred ship which travels.

Dusty sheets of paper
perversely twisted stride
rapidly to the engine room
fire in the water
the carriage of blood travels drunkenly.

I depart at night.
I sense an older age
in a song of sleep.
Pain, since it became pain,
relaxes backstage.
Outside, a supplicant, a magician.

The photograph is devoid of bones.
The bright sun combs the wood.
Fire in the air as guilt is vaporised
torn up by the roots.
I sleep
and the night becomes a thief.

Though the desert grows light
fear passes the night in the sand.
Elements of flame offered as a gift.
A self-taught sky.
Eternal.
The sun a wreath of blood.

I was scoured.
And my skin was blackened
by the whispering waters.
I, a graduate of the stars
with a bright shirt, hence the antagonism
a momento in my eyes.

The hand scratches pages
with red chalk
time is clothed in unrelated words
inclined towards savagery
which you baptise perception out of charity.

From a child and from a dead man
the dream is explained

blood is an asset
a dissipation
a company of murderers in an
abatoir, housed along with statues.

GOOD MORNING

A close landscape, an uneasy season, I wake, an early bird,
ochre shutters, I am like the past, you said good morning
- as if it was night - and it was dark on the skin, on
the membrane, on the epithelium: there, the split nail
you kept, a dry cough, a spasm of the body
and it is morning, sleep died, no, it wasn't Endymion
who lulled you, which lullaby arising, ascension,
time for a drink, you, old woman on the bed, you chew
on something invisible - you are a ghost - dream without facade,
a multicoloured cat with seven souls - the terror of seven floors -
heliophobe, you stretch, the day begins and showers
beneath the body's umbrella.

PROGRESSIVE LEVELS

Level 0 (White)

it is essential, the auxiliary exists.

You, yourself, seem to shudder.
The baggage:
Dry time on your fingers (and on your forehead).
Silent water in a flask.
The moon.

I untie myself trembling in freedom.

Level 1 (Yellow)

fortune and fortification.

The foam: "I hate untamed and unruly limbs".
I open the window to clear the foul stench.
Today I was blessed with this snow.
Now I carry a white shield.
What is this refusal when taut skin envelopes

Level 2 (Red)

omphalos, hestia.

Outside the night, inside, bad company.
As July grew more vast I thought we were moving towards the
sky
we were progressing.
We were eaten away by the damp earth I left on the bed.

Level 3 (Blue)

opening, exit.

The window a bulb.
The pillow a dreg of sleep I folded in love.
Wounded in an afternoon - a deep wound, a dream.
When young we eloped into a nightmare.

Level 4 (Green)

support, declining.

I am a needle.
Drop lost in a haystack, I sow a fragment of light.
I drink at full tilt.
These rivers are invisible, I drink.

Level 5 (Colourless)

it is essential, the auxiliary exists.

I encased you in a shell.
You dissolved blood in the sea.
You exist as a face.
I respect your lips.
I refused a ring which would split them.
If death was a man I could accept.

INVASION

You felt the light
as if it were escaping in the body
in a forgiving Mass where the oldest priest
continuously carries the torch of blood.

Light: only one syllable,
rust travels on somnabulistic winds
returning as clay - the footprint of God -
places gravity on the eyes.

Light calls out sharply to insects
with wings of sulphur to rise from the swamp
to blitz the vaporising face
with ancient mysteries from beneath the earth.

THE FLORA - THE FAUNA

The stomach, full of sun, chews over and over
the tongue, the skin you planted
on a honey-moon sky, to bear fruit
in a green and verdant place
where the growth of love
was swathed in blood bursting forth.

HOLY BREAD

In the past when the skies were tax free
how wildly you writhed
smeared unripe limbs with light.

In the past, that inability to mourn,
you'd spring up as if from sleep with a keen look,
the privilege of love on your face.

Now Mr Customs Man, how do you gauge the value of a body?
You collect embraces, going Dutch
constantly assessing the holy bread, a gift in return.

GRID

Many hide-aways call out to me
and take me with music in the darkness
as if I had knowledge,
alone in the room
with only the music
thinking
of all things, the before and the after.

I'm way too hot
I think without knowing.

What are these traces on the page?
What's a poet?
What's the material, the construction?
So many walls, so much work, too much heat.
And why?

I need to walk
a walk on the wild side
that doesn't exist.

I hit oblivion.

Another effort.

I open my eyes.
A rushing of wings.
It's not even worth a comparison.

The solution: the bath.
I like the whiteness inside.

I stare expectantly

into the geometric tiles.
I rest.
I think.

These prevalent axes
oiled from other fluids
those which are superfluous to us and load the joints
of the old threee dimensional compound.

The tears.

THE AMPHIBIAN WEAPON

The double-edged blade grew rotten - through weeping
in the guts
and the lights of the embryo were just sufficient
to salvage sanctuary.

The amphibian creature melted
in the liquids in the air
as if it were made of wax
and its wings became unstuck
its wings of blood
it had perfected the theft of liquid from the body
as if it wanted to fly.

When the time came
the weeping drenched the knife
and the canal shattered
the end was not instantaneous
it was only when the weapon split in two
one blade left for life
one blade left for death.

WHITE SHIRT

In my face I found myself
the image of a white shirt.

With many hands I hold myself like a rock
I blow music from the crack
to break the war
to leave.

PRESENT TENSE

This present tense offers me no recompense.

For long now it always vanishes
its glow is lost
is shattered.

As if this obsession animates me
makes me plough deeply into the earth
- exchanging weight with light
until it draws me
to a place where water and sound fuse beautifully
as if younger then
a remuneration
in the wide space of a bright moon
I move heavily into myself, into the open air,
into a time of rest.

There my lips perceive
my eyes recognise
and I, blind to the verb, delve in as a creator
as freely as the true are elected
things move, they are moved
into the archetypical shadow
into the mode of perception
with the ease
of the storm which deforms us
in the needle in the thorn
in the wild animal which explodes
in our eyes dispelling the evil eye
used to the sting
the most tenuous
in the hands which spread the present
in the sheets blowing in the wind

wrenching a texture from the sun.

'Oh'
You say.
You touched oblivion.
The switch in the stone pit is down.

Fate, the Mother of the Present.
The Father of the Present is Love.
Don't ask.

A MASS OF PEOPLE

The shadows grow deeper.
The future portends something funereal.
The heads of the great nations
enter alliance with the one or two who perish
number-stricken, the nations unleash their arrows of expansion
bodies are put to sleep behind mirrors
during days when light does not appear
the country slides underground
you dig and dig and find nothing
while new generations of reptiles multiply.

The earth: free, a jewel.
Suddenly becomes a down-trodden mass of people.

THE PATHOLOGY OF THE STONE

Brown-red huge innocent steps on the walk
barely forming a rough unwinding path
a stony place as it may be
filled with gravel and shards but
see how every midday touches at the ground
during your walks
as the light connects the spaces of your trek
boulders and corner stones lurk everywhere
perpendicular to the slates during the day they ramify
a bearing to the people who work the stone
an unconcerned July pervades the imaginary umbilical cord
a neutral observer of minerals
moving towards the quarries of the night
to unearth time from the sand.

THE POLLEN OF THE BODY

The night, diaphanous with incomprehensible diseases
shudders in spasm and burns the lips
waiting for the time of the white game
love is an unscrupulous worker
it gathers a wealth of pale dawn on the lips
it treats itself to the pollen of the body until
Sunday's voice says 'good morning' in tenderness
to the best old wine
to the best new water.

THE RULER OF THE CITY

The secret city
is in ruins like a flower of death.
All the men are dead.

By the castle over the water lies the open vein
of a silver deposit, the end of a small soul

but then

a lonely body of people
a woman's body
one woman advances alone, discmbowelled
she is the earth, an agony moves on.

It is summer and the moon is full
all among them whisper and mutter expecting the prize
it is almost the fall, the end of the summer.

Now tiny creatures from the neck of the city
cut loose deities
enmeshed like netted fish
the source and magnitude of the fire
paying no attention now to the ancient pollen
until

an angelic rainbow
the master of the sea
the visitor, brings hungry water
sun on the forehead and
the great man offers his condolences
- such dark excuses -
that destiny is the master of all.

42

The conqueror, he says, is guilty
he must be exiled at midnight

and as the summer sunset breaks
here lies the cause
a massive and revengeful storm
and here she is
at the gate
the mother
who cries for the son
who cries for the grandson

her lot was that cunning
treacherous man
- sadly -

and while the sand rises
this generation is scattered
inside the castle under a foreign sword

and the child
the ruler of the city
- who didn't make it -
burns out with the city.

A FAMILIAR WIND

When the familiar wind summoned me
back into my own power
I collapsed and shattered
as glass on trampled earth
and when the mirror cast away the mud
I choked inverted in the earth.

From the Spring which never came
I left the rights in your blood
a sword which severed my voice
I abandoned this in a rainy dawn.

RED - HOT WOMAN

I dream of a red-hot woman
in a hayloft with her legs open
to entwine our feet in the taste of the grape
the moon, though invisible, shines
my eyes creak as I write
in this way my love is ungrateful
woman, an arrogant water
but, to taste from those firm breasts.

I want whatever remains of God.

THE BURNING OF AUGUST

Egina, August 1992

An island dress
you spread your legs apart.

To have you next to me though you are not
for us to secretly exchange
the alphabet, the spelling of the Ancient Greek again,
to leave the night unbroken
and the same vocabulary in the morning
a splintered 'good morning' is articulated
for there is no balsam for the burning of August
save the expectation of the month going to rot.

Let's not allow the light to die over a burning.

SMOKE

The smoke of incense ascends
and is lost in the trunk of a tree.
The wood exhales and an angel is revealed
blond and shining in resin.

For years the smoke
nested in a woman
and enfolded her in a night-gown of the moon
in the stature and audacity of a boy.

VAPORISATION

The sunset burned our fingers
a hot light on our nails as they fired up
began to glow in mauve and rose.

With the soul's slow pace
quietly embraced we lost ourselves in the air.

PICNIC

The planet grows heavy with light
and you are enveloped by the aroma
as you bend to place a cloth on the grass
checking for a space in the clearing
to take a bite beneath the stars
the stars you prepared
the round
the diaphanous
the black.

IN THE NORTH

On the dark blue waves
in the North
where bas-relief waters resist
and the sapphire sea is on my back
there I encounter your form
as you glide invisibly towards me
with vowels full of light
(as if your heart still shone).

The air shivers with the morning's energy
your body a flame full of wings
your dress crackles in the air
as the zephyr breeze ruffles through it
until, so quickly,
you vanish
before I have time to kiss your lips.

Later, I think to myself, 'silence',
as another form drifts from the firmament.
See it,
it shakes up ashes and assembles its wings from the
earth.

33 RPM

I turn at 33 RPM,
my breathing sounds of vinyl.

You sleep heavily beside me
and I break into pieces.

The age is suddenly revealed
and there's rain, always the rain.

My eyes are disturbed
as they mark you as twenty years old.

THE SIMPLE METHOD

OF THREE

For my grandfather

THE SIMPLE METHOD OF THREE

If $\dfrac{A}{B} = \dfrac{\Gamma}{X}$ Then $X = \dfrac{B \times \Gamma}{A}$

A

MOORING

Searching for myself, how was I led astray?

A green sea alive with dolphins.
A drawing-room, a chandelier and printings of saints.
Nature rains with wet eyes
around the table creatures from the depths
converse.

A yard paved with geometrical tiling.
The mother, the water, the father.
The father, the water, the dust.

The gate resembles a pier
the waves break, the concrete breaks
huge boats arrive.
The father, the mother, the dust.

On the oars are vermin like stigmata.
Where is the mooring, the knot, the wave.

Searching for myself, how was I led astray?

YOU CANNOT CHOOSE

To Zefi Daraki and Byron Leontaris

What can I say?
I grew weary of staring at shadows
burned and empty paper -
drowned paper of the mountain.

Before me are bones dyed red
interlaced with severed limbs.

Perhaps here a demand was given
a choice!
I chose coral
the daisy of symbols.

You cannot choose.

Here is your life and here are the words.
Here are the words and peace.
Here and there and further.

What excuse, which Easter, which resurrection?
Where now is that pristine gold?

Unloving, the homeless, burning man lights a candle.

We all have our private angels.
The most foul angel is my own.

Between the sport and the profession
between the before and the after
like a fisherman absorbed by the end of the pier.
You fish and catch nothing.

You cannot choose.

Friends lead us down to the sea.
Their thoughts, their burning sweat unsettling us
sharp pain everywhere
on our tongues, our limbs, our chests.

We are in the narrow passes.
Already huge mountains expand.
We say the mountains, we say the sea.

You cannot choose.

DESCENDANT OF A DREAM
For Gerard de Nerval (1808-1855)

This January night
I watch a silhouette jumping from one tile to another
on the diaphanous roofs of les maisons de Valois
holding to the spouts and gutters
until with a deft leap he lands
on an adjacent balcony.

During this night *both black and white*
an inexplicable diffraction
as you shed images from the past.

During this night on the roofs of Valois
the soul
this rider of dreams
drifts backwards like an immaterial body.

We would like to believe that when the pain overflowed
into his guts
when disruptions and erysipelas
pushed his mind to analysis of ancient anxieties
he left the forms of eternal women in fertility.

From the allegory of Jenny Colon
to the shining of Marie Playel
Sylvie intervenes
sweet mother of the second life of sleep
from les Halles to the Vieille-Lanterne
the definitive Aurelia rises
the infinitely lost
a sacrifice to the noose of the narrator of the skies
to the divine descendant of dreams.
That night the cat remembers faces.

CASTAWAYS

The castaways watch the ship slowly sinking
until the peak of the mast perishes
they sail away, with the canvas full blown
on their second journey
the real quest
until over rolling waves they open the sail of momentum
gleaming and persistent bodies
they resist the grace of the depths
dropping their eyes in a salty drunkeness
pilgrims to an unknown longing
scarcely realising the poverty of their bodies
captives of the illusion of a journey
on the humble life-jacket of destiny.

CAFE

(for Kostas Papageorgiou)

A cup of coffee
as if in a still-life
but, on the forehead the white wolf,
inconspicuous in his grey garb,
white-toothed with a hidden knife
talking of candles of Resurrection
of Bengal lights and Byzantine icons
offering us breath and a warm hand
offering to encompass us deep within his body.

THE LITTLE SUBVERSIVE

I want you to make good progress
this is how I want you.
I have no wish to see you stumbling
only dragging your steps in the yard
in your dark jacket
feeling the passage of time.

As your progression goes well
I note
that deep in the core of your nail
you nurture a caress
and I think
that no one explained this to you
that you'd feel grief when this day came
when you
a Little Subversive
would want to melt the burning with one of your fingers
incisively with this tiny
and sensitive nail of yours.

YOUR HABITS

Your habitual faculty of perceiving
the slightest trace of water
in the rings of a felled tree.

Your habit of disparaging a conversation
- later - as if it was polluted
from within crevices of syllables.

Your habit of tasting
passions as if they were bright spices
succulent fruits which you formerly ignored.

Your habitual capacity of noticing the merest look
and sinking the scenario in withered leaves
in the three dimensions of vision.

These habits of yours.

THE UNEXPECTED

Why so suddenly could I see!

Forgive me I will guard this memory.

Through a crack in the mirror I found a woman to study
deeply drawn from a rusty dictionary from the 'A' of Anthropos
through to the 'Z' of Zenith.

A disruption, an agitation of the whole body.
My only concern until then exactly the same image
  but reversed.
This love creating the ideal partner.

I stood stunned and consented to this new thought:
I edged around my life reaching the compassion of a child.
But what a danger.
Repetitions will never become the rule of nature.

THE LANDSCAPE

The day collapsed and faded
without a flourish
without a sound
like a wild animal scarred in the breast.

On the brown cell strewn earth
beneath the rocks a mossy fuzz
a snake-skin whip thrown
from a gloved hand
all like the reflection of a vast sea.

*

It was then that the weird Sirocco blew
and swept the limbs of the stars away
as if from the depths of the sea
a wild voice arose
the established form of nature sighed deeply.

Distant seashores shuddered
and the seasons' thin figures cracked
each one clutching their lot
in their fists with such a strength
that the entire landscape
shed its warm colours on the ground.

THE RETURN

The wind blew and shook the gates of the world
white birds lashed their wings to move inside
but the gates were strong and the keys were hidden.

With all the strength in the tips of his fingers
he holds firmly to the banister
he speaks the dialect of air.

He doesn't know when with arrogance
the stagnant waters of midday will invade.

Had he ever paid them attention when he returned
soaked to the bone
with his mouth stuttering seed
his face contracted
a sick saint?

At twenty years old with such an eternal spark
how could he hear
the eye-lids flickering
the internal sounds which govern
the gigantic phosphorous insect.

But he returned to the cave at a steady pace
to where the dull light made the walls pallid
where he hardly discerned the clutter of the old animals
old animals indelibly engraved with death stones
deeply in the northern lights of his soul.

IN A DREAM I AM A SHADOW

In a dream I am a shadow
in a light boat
on gleaming waters
my mouth is dry
as I listen:

You know it. Why don't you look?

I lean over and I perceive you
painted sunlight on the surface of the sea.

What do you remember?

Ash scattered in an inaccessible room.
Ash
and the blackness
an adroit blackness
with its cape shining.

Tell me. Tell me, who am I?

Your blood is ousted and spreads.
Your veins fill with a salty light
thorns which grow in the ground
thorns which grow in the flesh
your blood is ousted and spreads.

Do you see me? Can you see me?

You no longer possess sound.
You withdraw the image into pale light
you vanish leaving my shadow in a void.

THE LIGHT OF THE WORLD

Now I see you.
I turn and recognise you on the wet surface.

Wherever you are, come closer
now that I understand
you shine from the floor of the sea
whole
great light.

Your flaxen glow
your aroma of joy
your inner splendour
your brilliance
my syllables unfold.

I cast my shadow and you vanish
your perpetual form is dislocated
and flows deep within me
a great revelation
the light of the world.

THE LEAF AN UNFADING NOTE

The leaf an unfading note
a cold hand on it
the earth is the most pale
the speechless
the hour I await you.

An elaborate seal on the chest
an unsigned letter
the body leaves
an unexpected
soft creeping darkness.

The wreckless decision I demanded of you
in the depths of joy
in the eyes
in the face.

Love is the place you resist.

EVERY DAY BETRAYED

The house is closed.
It is neither Monday, nor Tuesday
There is no day in this house.

> She laughs casting a golden fan
> thinking of fine theatrical movements.
> I wonder if she remembers the poverty in which they found her
> now, which air, which fan
> the same head as then
> the same look, the same fringe -

> *betrayed on the same day*

It is neither Wednesday, nor Thursday
it is not Friday.
There is no day in this house.

> - She suffers and suspects
> un-nameable pains appearing.
> She thinks 'the scars of sleep'
> touching to the jewels around her throat
> she imagines a long journey
> in the future, to travel, to leave -

> *betrayed on the same day*

In the end it is not Saturday
nor is it Sunday
no day can exist in this house.

> - How can all this dust be embraced
> how can this rotting body be lifted.
> Eventually through lime the sand of fire

will be raised
a new mask will be completed
she will touch it with the tips of her fingers
in fear of breaking it
the day will shatter
in marble -

Everyday betrayed

BEYOND

Hands open expansively
in a drunken embrace, transmitted
like a contagious disease.

On the sands you maintain that
the antibodies come at midnight with the full moon.

But here beaches don't exist
only predatory birds, thunder and forests,
there are insoluble riddles, like,
the figs are poison and the wash-tub is an urn.

The place is unbaptised.
The place of Beyond and Above
the window of one use only.

WE MEET

You pass close by me and I am at a loss.
Wondering how you can be so near and how it happens
this reeling and twining in the white embryo of sleep
and for you to be only you.

I open my arms for you.

If you leave I think and think about the night
a sheet allowed to fall alone
I note pictures which recognise me and I see.

I remember the island, the leaf of a fig-tree, bodies embraced
a red handkerchief left in a pot
your absent mindedness in summer.

I open my arms for you.

In your town at midday
I remember the earth and the sea
- then the forgotten star I boasted of -

I know a language which becomes us.
I know how to communicate.
I know how to speak to you.

I open my arms for you.

I give you my man-made river-bed.

PIANO

(For Katerina Anghelaki A. Rooke)

A wooden piano
sinks slowly
the black and white keys
the notes and wet semi-tones
in the depths with a mass of plankton
on top
is a protective umbrella
a body casts its shadow
the body of a woman
an umbilical cord
a love which didn't exist
the beginning in the wind
the end in the water.

RORROH*

Rorroh, her name a comb of bone
Rorroh, a stitched wound
every day sees
an empty disease in her palm.

Rorroh, a proud being
a tight white smile.
Rorroh, an upright almond tree
an air and echo of metal.

Rorroh, a woman of the palace
with precious gems in her cache
she dances writhes and undulates.

Rorroh, a snake girl
only to be loved in reverse.

*Rorroh: Horror written in reverse

CRIB-SHEET

It is quiet tonight
wreathed in the smell of children.

Beneath the roof is silence which breaks and spreads
abolishing the duty and the body
empty hair and empty eyes.

A crib-sheet from the past to the future
folded
it spells out clearly:

The blood unhealed, unhealed.

QUAGMIRE

Her eyes wide open and ashen
her shoulders folded and distant
her waist wreathed and indefinable
this I remember from all that I've lived.

*

And it was a summer day
which didn't strike the mind as summer
, in a year that quivered
running in the sewers day by day
by the metro with the mice and rats.

The whole year was a lake from another epoch
but aside from that I think I met her there -
in a wet shelter
in a haunted room
in a room with too much rust.

Since then much time has passed
the snow has melted
the marble has become a mirror
the tiles gleam
and a piercing light, as of the soul, descended
from the clouds, from the blue of the sky
and the room grew tainted with the cold colours of death
which only she
- and perhaps not even she -
had ever perceived.
The place became a mausoleum
obviously only to those who recognised it
and to those who passed by
thinking that the dream

had devoured them -
for such was the power and anticipation
that the place was alight with tension and all forms of energy
you'd think if you touched the walls you'd burn, but...

*

I entered it and grew bold
I wanted to see and lit a candle
I saw though the candle both flickered and shone
that all the doors bore scratches
which I tried to fathom
- for it was a letter -
this was no judgement, no consequence of an upheaval
resulting in the engraving of these symbols
it was as though some video-tape played
through the false ceiling
but I was not reassured
there was a real ceiling adorned with a mural, of course,
there was Achilles and Patroklos and there
were forms resembling massive snakes
there was also a zone like a swamp
like deep muddy wet-lands
and there was the word 'quagmire'
reflected in the waters
which I had to read in reverse
then I saw him before me, full of life
as if he himself had seen the ghost of his father
and held your face in his hands.

It was then that my courage grew sufficiently
to try to decipher
but in vain
for they were only scratches
they were scratches
and you have been gone for a long time now.

DECEMBER

December is a damaging month
I close my eyes and it takes advantage.

No harvest this year, nothing
compared to last year or the year before.

This month encapsulates the crowded world
trouble, silence, distance.

Visible actions are omitted.
My back against
a non-existent wall.

The courage of the evening is consolation
the mud, the grass.

The integral government of the month.

SALT

Now, here is the sea, moving in from the depths
an extravagant deposit of twilight
the coming rain scatters the flavour of an untouchable
dream.

Now, here is the sea, turbulent and wild
and the skies flash fire
on the body of infinite salinity
as it grows from the waves of flame.

Now, here is the sea, debilitated from
                    its exhausting effort
it casts an eternal murmuring
before the same cycle resumes at dawn.

Now, here is the sea, pounding holding heaven's beam,
the dawn comes sruggling for air, and it calms,
obeying the call of the salt.

THE INVISIBLE MAN

The Invisible Man, before becoming invisible, thought: 'I don't want to be conspicuous, I don't want to exist, consequently I'll hide, I will become latent, I will crawl.'

And this is how it came to pass.

From an initial haziness he became an undercurrent, nestling, smuggled away, until in the end he succeeded. He vanished, he became extinct.

Then he lived clandestinely, beyond notice, he put the only dream of his life into action: to exist beyond visibility.

Being imperceptible, non existent to others - he could walk invisible through all the places he had dreamed of. Initially he observed and scrutinised he began to touch, you might say supervise, those places he thought formerly he could only reach by imagination.

Following considerable contemplation and analysing their structure, their particularities, their fragmentary images - how reality worked - only then did he decide to intervene.

And so in this way the Invisible Man, not only indiscernible to others but quite literally absent, found himself in a position, with a little projection, a little interference, to transform a shot on the crossbar into a goal, to help, minimally but timely a vaulter in his final effort, to transform a vicious stabbing into a superficial graze, to include an apparently insignificant - but effectively determining term in a contract to accelerate the actions of an akward lover, in short to manipulate reality in all kinds of ways, but, always according to his own sense of morality, his own exclusive preferences. He became a bizarre referee, a regulator in the fates of others.

The weak point in the actions of the Invisible Man centred on the verissimilitude of his indefinable mediations. If the flow of events manifestly changed the whole scenario would shatter, it would become a caricature, a fiasco.

So, the Invisible Man began to act with the precision of a surgeon, he analysed, checked the impulses the imperceptible incursions, he was cautious with his inpalpable intrusions. He learned how to move carefully, he was cautious never to be caught by the eye, especially by the subjects playing a particularly important role in an event, finally he became invisible in his invisibility.

This went on for a long time. At the outset the Invisible Man enjoyed himself immensely. At last his life had found a meaning. But with the passing of time he began to realise that something had gone wrong. The precision, the necessity of his own actions the fact that his interventions had to be both concrete and infinitessimal began to wear him down. His meticulous attention to forcing his intrusions to appear natural, as if events unfurled with ease, killed him.

He had begun to set programmes, to build up catalogues, to estimate the value of his interventions. The interventions had become a routine. His hands were tired, he was in a hurry, he became increasingly slovenly.

The decay did not take long to come. An ungainly movement and the entire edifice collapsed. And then the Invisible Man, who had become invisible for good, said:

'I want to be visible, I want to exist, therefore, I will not hide, I will not be latent, I will not crawl.'

But it was too late, no one could see him anymore.

...333...333...333...

And without overdosing
you grew accustomed to me
as an essential element in the concoction of time
plus the minus which divided us in three.

CHARLES' SLEIGH

Little Charles' sleigh races
leaving wintery tracks on the ground.

The sun gleams on its metal runners
as the child grips firmly to the reins
to pull back on the acceleration.

But Little Charles' sleigh takes off downhill
he swerves from his course
he skids, the blades cannot withstand the centrifugal force.

The headlong, dizzying ride continues
traversing the winter mountains of America
until at last the sleigh derails,
and the boy is catapulted
and lands harshly on the frozen ground.

Later
after a prolonged search they find him
  half-dead
and when they succeed
  in bringing him round,
Little Charles half opens his eyes
and murmurs only one word

      'ROSEBUD'

THE MUSEUM

The cause: the museum of childhood.

He sits cross-legged and jokes with two childhood friends.

The place: the town of Catalonia which the great Gaudi embellished.

Looking then at the old paintings he perceives
        that he passed through the classical period unharmed,
how even from childhood his hand lead of its own volition,
rendering the illness of his father
through to the smile of a young girl-friend.

Beside him his fellow-traveller with the waxed moustache,
upright, haughty, the inventor of a new language
with a shoulder wounded by the blue bullet of Garcia.
The poet follows tacitly.

*

All three together in the same printing.
That of God lying stretched out
- not that one of Toledo but the more Eastern one -
operated on (for who knows what disease).
All three on the canvas in a corner low on the left,
they are hardly discernible
in the upturned oval flemish mirrors,
staring alone
at the infinite brush strokes of life.

THE BOARDS

You tree who masquerade endlessly
from which chasm in your wood does your fruit flower?
Through which fissure in your nature does the light enter?

You, progenitor, what ancient stories do your members articulate
which mythical heroes quiver in your splinters?
How many venomous thorns are implanted in your vulnerable body?

You tree, at once different and the same,
you who transform your foliage to your own image
how many lies do you direct on the burst planks of your theatre.

MUSIC

The record shattered from continuous playing,
the viny evaporated, the melodies poured into the room
and glued themselves on the posters of the singers,
the Classical, the Dionysian, the Suicidal,
until finally they became rooted
- coloured melodies of death -
on the body of the Survivor
to torture his life of silk for ever.

SCHOOL SHOW

The show opened with drawings on the blackboard
with their geometrical angles and inverted images
in classes red veins pulsed
attacking the trivialities of their classmates
of the petty and mean public
forced to absorb -
that public which is comprised of need and venom.

OLD FRIEND

My old friend changed
becoming a third person
somehow appearing angry
with mute teasing movements
in different clothes in which he shivered.

The summoning which was formerly a provocation has become an ease
of sorts these days
the signs of distance all covert yet still so discernible.

There, particularly
under his shirt,
there, precisely at the naval,
it seems that fatigue takes form
regulating his new life.

THE ANGUISH OF THE POLITICIAN

The anguish of the politician is an experience of the underworld.

It's not so much the visit
but the death shroud the visitor carries on his return.

The anguish of the politician is a wild chilled animal,
a gross corpse with no visible wounds.

TEN SECONDS

The suspense is unbearable
muscles tense
the body as taut as a drawn bow.

The cheering has subsided
only deep breathing and the flow of the body
as the silver winds up nerves
and shimmers on the wet track.

Black eyes defined by two white lines
are focused on the lane.
Time stops, an assuring assistant.
Silence.

*

When the crack was heard
the body was unleashed
and the adrenalin flowed
the absolute racecourse
the race of one breath
in ten inexorable seconds.

THE LOOK OF SEP

(For Georgio Delikari)

In the November of '74
when sweat was sweat
at high noon
he saw her approaching from the left
commended by the short man
that eternal lover.

Diverse images flashed through his mind like lightning
until the curve was rounded.
Perhaps it was the rancid smell of the old kitchen,
his love of damp rooms
or the tiled yard of Drapetsona.

Perhaps it was the images
which primed his body to such a position of distortion
that no terms could hope to describe.

The touch of the leather was sweet
and the result certain.

Sep simply looked.

IN THE LAND OF IMAGES

I found a narrow slit in the screen
and I quickly wormed my way in.

The projectors burned
I was really far too hot.

I meticulously began to remove the pictures
and pile up the invisible burning pixels next to me.

When I finished
I folded up my control and put it on top.

The entrails put on a play.
I think it was a comedy of situations.

Then I took a bout of fever
I don't recall how this came about.

Dead tired I returned by the same route.

MONDAY

*even the greatest ship can be sunk
by the smallest rock*

Yesterday's dark poisons
taken from a forgotten land
they extracted a piece
a piece alight
and the place stunk of salinity
until from within the chasm
an old wolf with ashen hair appeared.

He began to write in the sand with his snout
the messages of tomorrow
where we would be, who we would see, when we would leave
- then he lay down on the ground
and carefully began doing his accounts.

TUESDAY

The car rolled slowly stuck in first gear
I knew it
it will pass now the heart pumping the foot grinding
the blue car with the small flags
with a battered silver bumper
- if you could see the tracks -
the skid-burn of the tyres a blurred letter
rolling out behind terrorising the world
a rhythm of breath and of asphalt
where the weight of the passenger leads to the end.

WEDNESDAY

A week scarred from the outset.
Today a distinction.
At night the sound of the mountains.

An old anticipated picture.
A perplexity, a certainty.

I have witnessed the reflections in the depths and I know
how passion becomes a poem and I know its path
to find a secret passage
where the weight of the sky is heavy.

This is the place where I expect you
to wash me in your ancient silences
with your own intimate and calculated movements.

This is the place where I will thank you for the hours
you imagined your great adornment shining in me.

THURSDAY

A journey through thr old days, sir.
A journey which lacerates the afternoon.
A journey which swallows up the kilometres.

It's unnecessary to look out the window, sir
nor to steal looks from the mirrors.
Look in front of you at the speedometre at the
steering wheel, look
a profile quartered
from there you understand, sir

that the night before Holy Communion
- the filthy night of the body -
that in such a place
you received redemptive blood
fortunately ignoring everything, sir
fortunately ignoring everything.

FRIDAY

Yesterday, Hank as well.
I've already stated: 'hard week'.
It had already tolerated a lot.
But the other?

In Mileas of Pilion or in Bizii
in Rafina or in Lagonisi
the same saliva dries
on a small corner of the night.

SATURDAY

Who will introduce the Bettina Fravassili of
                    our lives?
Who will define the future of such love?

It seems that only when the thimble of this world
                    overflows
when we have rid ourselves of all family
                    burdens
ignoring every circumstance
the scares that cut our nerves
then uninhibited we will camp in the mines of
                    our souls
within our own personal arches
listening to the sounds of metal
to a black swallow taking flight.

(Bettina Fravassili; the last tragic love of the well known
Greek writer Viizinos).

SUNDAY

reconstruction of tissue

It is already late.
The last day passes away
as we sit on the diaphanous shore
around the roughly made
fasting table
we've soaked to the bone the whole week
we order time
from the stocks of the body.

Saintly inertia on the face of the sand
a salutory insomnia.
The singular numbers of nature.
We, new-born cells worn out through long passage
silently receive communion in the dampness of the evening.